To Parents and Teachers:

We hope you and the children will enjoy reading this story in English and Spanish. It is simply told, but not *simplified,* so that both versions are quite natural. However, there is lots of repetition for practicing pronunciation, for helping develop memory skills, and for reinforcing comprehension.

At the back of the book, there is a simple picture dictionary with key words as well as a basic pronunciation guide to the whole story.

Here are a few suggestions for using the book:

- First, read the story aloud in English to become familiar with it. Treat it like any other picture book. Look at the drawings, talk about the story, the characters, and so on.

- Then look at the picture dictionary and repeat the key words in Spanish. Make this an active exercise. Ask the children to say the words out loud instead of reading them.

- Go back and read the story again, this time in English and Spanish. Don't worry if your pronunciation isn't quite correct. Just have fun trying it out. If necessary, check the guide at the back of the book, but you'll soon pick up how to say the Spanish words.

- When you think you and the children are ready, try reading the story in Spanish. Ask the children to say it with you. Only ask them to read it if they seem eager to try. The spelling could be confusing and discourage them.

- Above all, encourage the children, and give them lots of praise. They are usually quite unselfconscious, so let them be children and play act, try out different voices, and have fun. This is an excellent way to build confidence for acquiring foreign language skills.

First edition for the United States and Canada published 1996 by Barron's Educational Series, Inc.
Text © Copyright 1996 by b small publishing, Surrey, England
Illustrations © Copyright 1996 by Alex de Wolf
Address all inquiries to: Barron's Educational Series, Inc., 250 Wireless Boulevard, Hauppauge, New York 11788
ISBN-13: 978-0-8120-6580-0   ISBN-10: 0-8120-6580-8   Library of Congress Catalog Card Number 95-53764
Printed in Shenzhen Wing King Tong Paper Product Co. Ltd. Shenzhen Guangdong China
Date of Manufacture: April 2010   19 18 17 16 15 14 13 12 11

I want my banana!

¡Quiero mi plátano!

Mary Risk

Pictures by Alex de Wolf
Spanish by Rosa Martín

BARRON'S

Monkey has lost his banana.

El mono perdió su plátano.

He's sad.

Está triste.

"Would you like an orange?"
says Python.

"¿Quieres una naranja?"
dice la pitón.

"It's nice and juicy."

"Es buena y jugosa."

"No, thanks," says Monkey.

"No, gracias," dice el mono.

"I want my banana."

"Quiero mi plátano."

"Have some nuts," says Parrot.

"Toma unas nueces," dice el loro.

"No, thanks," says Monkey.

"No, gracias," dice el mono.

"I only like bananas."

"Sólo me gustan los plátanos."

"Have a pineapple," says Hyena.

"Toma una piña," dice la hiena.

"It's very sweet."

"Es muy dulce."

"No, thanks," says Monkey.

"No, gracias," dice el mono.

"I just want my banana."

"Sólo quiero mi plátano."

"Come here, little monkey,"
says Tiger.

"Ven aquí, monito," dice el tigre.

"I'll give you your banana."

"Yo te daré tu plátano."

But Monkey sees his banana.

Pero el mono ve su plátano.

And he grabs it just in time!

¡Y lo agarra justo a tiempo!

Monkey's happy now.

El mono está contento ahora.

"Bananas are best," he says.

"Los plátanos son lo mejor," dice.

Pronouncing Spanish

Don't worry if your pronunciation isn't quite correct. The important thing is to be willing to try. The pronunciation guide here is based on the Spanish accent used in Latin America. Although it cannot be completely accurate, it certainly will be a great help:

• Read the guide as naturally as possible, as if it were English.

• Put stress on the letters in *italics* e.g. past*el*.

If you can, ask a Spanish speaking person to help and move on as soon as possible to speaking the words without the guide.

Note: Spanish adjectives usually have two forms, one for masculine and one for feminine nouns. They often look very similar but are pronounced slightly differently, e.g., **jugoso** and **jugosa** (see the word list below).

Words Las palabras

lahs pah *lah* brahs

monkey

el mono

ehl *moh* noh

python

la pitón

lah peeh *tohn*

parrot
el loro
ehl *loh* roh

banana
el plátano
ehl *plah* tah noh

hyena
la hiena
lah ee *eh* nah

orange
la naranja
lah nah *rahn* hah

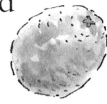

nuts
las nueces
lahs noo *eeh* sehs

tiger
el tigre
ehl *tee* greh

pineapple
la piña
lah *pih* nya

sad
triste
treehs teh

happy
contento/contenta
cohn *tehn* toh/cohn *tehn* tah

nice
bueno/buena
bway noh/*bway* nah

delicious
delicioso/
deliciosa
deh lih *see oh* soh/deh lih *see oh* sah

sweet
dulce
dool seh

juicy
jugoso/jugosa
hoo *goh* soh/hoo *goh* sah

would you like a...
¿quieres un/una...?
kee *eh* rehs uhn/uhna...?

have a...
toma un/una...
toh mah uhn/uhna...

I want a...
quiero un/una...
kee *eh* roh uhn/uhna

A simple guide to pronouncing this Spanish-language story

El mono perdió su plátano.
ehl *moh* noh pehr di *oh* suh
plah tah noh

Está triste.
ehs *tah treeh*s teh

**"¿Quieres una naranja?" dice
la pitón.**
kee *eh* rehs uhna nah *rahn* hah
dee seh lah peeh *tohn*

"Es buena y jugosa."
ehs *bway* nah eeh hoo *goh* sah

"No, gracias," dice el mono.
noh *grah* see ahs *dee* seh ehl *moh*
noh

"Quiero mi plátano."
kee *eh* roh mee *plah* tah noh

**"Toma unas nueces," dice
el loro.**
toh mah oo nahs *noo eeh* sehs *dee*
seh ehl *loh* roh

"Son deliciosas."
sohn del lih see *oh* sahs

"No, gracias," dice el mono.
noh *grah* see ahs *dee* seh ehl *moh*
noh

"Solo me gustan los plátanos."
soh loh meh *guh*s tahn lohs *plah*
tah nohs

**"Toma una piña," dice la
hiena.**
toh mah uhna *pih* nya, *dee* seh
lah ee *eh* nah

"Es muy dulce."
ehs mwee *dool* seh

"No, gracias," dice el mono.
noh *grah* see ahs *dee* seh ehl *moh*
noh

"Solo quiero mi plátano."
soh loh kee *eh* roh mee *plah* tah
noh

**"Ven aquí, monito" dice
el tigre.**
behn ah *kee* moh *nih* toh *dee* seh
ehl *tee* greh

"Yo te daré tu plátano."
yoh teh dah *reh* uhn *plah* tah noh

Pero el mono ve su plátano.
peh roh ehl *moh* noh veh suh *plah*
tah noh

¡Y lo agarra justo a tiempo!
eeh loh ah *gah* rah *hoo*s toh ah *tee*
ehm poh

El mono está contento ahora.
ehl *moh* noh ehs *tah* cohn *tehn* toh
ah *oh* rah

**"Los plátanos son lo mejor,"
dice.**
lohs *plah* tah nohs sohn loh
meh *hor dee* seh